I0075837

I WANT TO BE

DEBT FREE

By DYKE SURINE

TABLE OF CONTENTS

INTRODUCTION

This is a guide and a teaching tool, to help individuals manage their finances and to become debt free. To be free of every day worry, money, and how the bills are going to be paid. I will be using biblical scriptures and known practical principles. This guide is good for anyone's income, regardless of their situation. I believe as Christians, GOD expects us to use His word and apply it to our lives even in finances, and to rid ourselves to the bondage of money. Debt and the burden of bills can weigh heavily on our hearts, and prevent you from leading a happy and fruitful life. It can also affect our physical lives as well, leading to extreme stress and high blood pressure.

Unfortunately we all need money to survive and exist in this world. They say; "money doesn't buy happiness," but it sure can make life a whole lot easier. We do have to be careful in being caught up in how we acquire it. The bible says; "For the love of money is the root of all kinds of evil. Some people, eager for money, have wandered from the faith and pierced themselves with much grief." (I Timothy 6:10 NIV) Remember this; money in itself is not evil. It is the love of it and how we acquire it. Second of all Ecclesiastes 5:10 states.

Whoever loves money never has money enough; whoever loves wealth is never satisfied with his income. This too is meaningless (NIV). So keep your lives free from the love of money and to be content with what you have, because GOD has said. "Never will I leave you; never will I forsake you." (Hebrews 13:5 NIV) The road to financial freedom is not easy. It is going to require discipline and hard work. Do not get discouraged, stay focused, and it will happen. Just believe in yourself. For the bible says; "And my GOD will meet all my needs according to His glorious riches in Christ Jesus." (Philippians 4:19 NIV) So we must be patient and not rush into things that get us in financial disarray. The bible says; "Dishonest money dwindles away, but he who gathers money little by little makes it grow." (Proverbs 13:11 NIV) The bible also states; "Whoever can be trusted with very little can also be trusted with much, and whoever is dishonest with very little will also be dishonest with much." (Luke 16:10 NIV)

You may ask; "why do I want to be debt free?" Well I do think that the average person does not enjoy paying bills, or to be constantly in debt to others. The bible says; "the rich rule over the poor, and the borrower is servant to the lender." (Proverbs 22:7 NIV) It is important that we pay our bills, and that we pay them on time!

Even the bible speaks of this; give everyone what you owe him: If you owe taxes, pay taxes, if revenue, then revenue; if respect, then respect; if honor, then honor. (Romans 13:7 NIV) It continues in verse 8 by saying; "owe no man anything, but to love one another; for he that loves another has fulfilled the law." (KJV) We also want to achieve a high credit score. For Christians I believe that this helps to make for a stronger witness and it shows responsibility. For even Jesus paid his bills and taxes. After Jesus and his disciples arrived in Capernaum, the collectors of the two drachma tax came to Peter and asked, "Doesn't your teacher pay the temple tax?" "Yes He does," he replied. Then Jesus said; "So that we may not offend them, go to the lake and throw out your line. Take the first fish you catch; open its mouth and you will find a 4-drachma coin. Take it and give it to them for my tax and yours." (Matthew 17:24 & 27 NIV) Let it be known: that the wicked borrow and do not repay, but the righteous give generously. (Psalm 37:21 NIV)

CHAPTER 1 "THE BUDGET"

The first thing we need to do is set up a budget. This budget will be on a weekly paycheck. If you get paid every two weeks, then divide your paycheck in half. If you get paid once a month, then divide your paycheck by 4. This particular budget discussed, is based on averages. The average work week is 41 hours. The average wage per hour is $23.00. You may say "I do not make nearly $23.00 per hour. I only make $12.00 per hour." But your spouse makes $11.00 per hour. So together you make $23.00 per hour. The average yearly income is

$49,600. So for this budget we are going to say that there is $800.00 a week coming in to the household.

You may ask; "How do I start a budget?" If you are a pay as you go kind of person, in other words, when the bill comes in, you wait till your paycheck comes and then you pay it. Well once you pay it, with your next paycheck, also set aside ¼ of the money needed to pay this bill. As other bills come in do the same for each. So the next time these bills come in you can pay it right away. You need to do this with all your monthly bills until they are all set up on a budget. This may take a month or two to get this all started.

So let us determine what we are going to set up on the budget. It is not necessary to budget every single thing we spend our money on. Basically you should budget your monthly or long term expenses, or ones that you have a hard time gathering the money for. Monthly expenses would be electric, car, house, phone, or credit cards. Long term expenses would be insurance or taxes something that is paid every 3 or 6 months or even once a year. Items that you would not budget would be weekly expenses like groceries, gasoline, or even donations. But by not budgeting weekly expenses you must remember to have money set aside to cover them. Now weekly expenses can be controlled in the event that you have a short paycheck. By not buying as many groceries, going less places to save gas, or do not eat out that week. Your monthly or long term expenses generally cannot be controlled. You can cut back on some expenses or even eliminate some such as cable or satellite TV, if you have 2 or 3 vehicles, could you live on 1 or 2. Try to find cheaper insurance rates. Try to cut on your electrical usage by keeping your thermostat lower on heat or higher on cool. All these little things add up.

Budgeting is done by separating specific amount of money into a separate area or container. This can be done in different ways.

#1 The Envelope System. Each envelope is labeled with the name of the expense or bill. Then the budgeted amount of money each week is placed inside. After one month or 4 weeks it is taken out and used to pay the bill that has come in. The bill is paid by check, money order, electronically, or taken to the place of business. Another way to do this would be to use play money in place of real money. This keeps your money in the bank. The only drawback is that you deal in dollars only and not cents and could have a tendency to be less accurate.

#2 The Paper System. This is the one that I use. I highly recommend this way as it is very accurate because you do deal with dollars and cents. Use 8 x 10 pieces of paper. Each paper is to be used for each expense. You will need to have two sets of papers. One set of papers represents all the expenses that you have or that you want to set up a budget for. The other set is to represent your money on hand, such as weekly paychecks, (spending money) and savings. I have one for my house; I call it the house fund. It is used to purchase things for my home or for home improvements. I have separate ones for my paycheck and my wife's paycheck. Our left over money from our weekly paychecks goes into the savings and house fund. I divide the money this way. I put 70% into savings and 30% into the house fund. For example: Let us say I have $10.00 left over from the week. So 70% of $10.00 would $7.00 and this goes into the savings. Now 30% of $10.00 would be $3.00 and this goes into the house fund.

So on each paper draw lines vertically or length wise to divide it into columns. I make mine 4 columns. In the first column write down the name of the expense and underneath that write the word balance. Each week write in the dollar amount designated to that expense. Each week keep writing in the dollar amount and adding it to the previous amount already there. When the bill comes in and you pay it, subtract the amount paid from what you have. If you do not have enough money, take from another expense where you may have extra or from your paycheck or savings. If you have some left over, keep it where it is or transfer it to your savings.

#3 Electronically. You can set up a system on your phone or computer to keep track that way. This system will allow you to be very accurate also because you can deal with dollars and cents.

So let us set up our budget.

House Payment: $1,030.00/mo. /4 = $257.50/wk. or Rent: $700.00/mo. /4 = $175.00/wk.

Car $420.00/mo. /4 = $105.00/wk.

Insurance/Car & House $55.00/wk.

Electric $50.00/wk.

Phone & Internet $30.00/wk.

Credit Cards $28.25/wk.

Miscellaneous (Medical, Club Dues, Car Repairs, or whatever else) $50.00/wk.

Total payout is $575.75/wk. with house or $493.25 with rent. Left over after payout is $224.25/wk. or $306.75/wk. (rent).

What is left over must pay for groceries, gas, eating out, & other little odds & ends. It shows that there is just not that much wiggle room left for anything else. For the remainder of this discussion we will just use the house payment, not the rent. If you were debt free, there would be no house, car, or credit card payments. This would reduce the payout to $185.00/wk. and left over would be $615.00/wk. That sure sounds sweet to me! How about you?

You should have a 3 column ledger book to keep track of all your spending and deposits that are made in your account. You can purchase these books at Office Depot, Office Max or Staples. There is room in these ledgers for other columns. My ledger is set up as so. Column #1, the date, column #2 check number, column #3, description of transaction, column #4, check mark, column #5, payment or withdrawal, column #6, deposit, and column #7, balance. Each week I view my account on line to see what has cleared my account. That is where column #4, check mark, comes into play. When I see that something that I wrote in column #3, description of transaction, has been taken out of my account, then I make a check mark in column #4 on that line. That tells me that this money is no longer in my account. Make sure you keep all your receipts so you record all of your spending in your ledger and subtract the dollar amounts from your expense and paycheck papers.

CHAPTER 2 STEP #1
TITHING

We need to tithe a portion of our income to GOD. The bible says; "Remember this; whoever sows sparingly will also reap sparingly, and whoever sows generously will also reap generously. Each man should give what he has decided in his heart to give, not reluctantly or under compulsion, for GOD loves a cheerful giver." (2 Corinthians 9:6 & 7 NIV)

Let us look at this from a different point of view. Let us say you wanted to invest some money, but you were not sure of what would be a good investment, or a sure fire investment. After all we really do not like losing money to especially poor decisions. Then you find someone, who you completely trust, who says to you that they can guarantee, that if you invest in this particular company or stock, that your money, beyond the shadow of a doubt, will definitely multiply above and beyond what you could ever imagine. How much would you be willing to invest? Well I can tell you this that GOD is the greatest investment you could ever make.

CHAPTER 3 STEP #2 EMERGENCY FUND

We need to save $1,000.00 for emergencies. Maybe your car needs some work, or a new kitchen appliance is needed and you do not have the money. Maybe you need to go to the doctor. This is for whatever the emergency is. So you will not have to use a credit card or dig into your designated bill money. Now it has been determined by the budget that you have $224.00 left over, and that is needed to buy groceries, gas, and whatever else you need. When the week is over and your next paycheck has come in you may have a little money left over. Maybe it is only $20.00, give or take. Whatever the amount is, this goes towards the $1,000.00 emergency fund. Remember this $20.00 x 52 weeks is $1,040.00. So it may take a few months to save $1,000.00. Try not to spend all of your paycheck. Try to cut corners wherever you can. Bring your lunch to work instead of buying lunch out. Experts say that the average lunch is $13.00, x 5 is $65.00 a week. Like I said this is not going to be easy!

CHAPTER 4 STEP #3 CREDIT CARDS

Step #3 is a huge step and perhaps one that is going to take quite a bit of time. We must pay off all credit cards. While in the process of doing this, you must try and refrain from continual credit card usage. If an emergency arises where you need to purchase something, then use your $1,000.00 emergency fund. But you always need to replenish it. The object is we need to avoid and pay off debt. You are also working towards a change in your thinking and buying habits. The average credit card debt is $5,700.00, with a 17.61% interest rate. If you only make the minimum payment it will take 17 years to pay it off. If you have multiple cards, well who knows how long all that will take to pay off. If you do not make at least the minimum payment by the due date, the credit card companies add on a late fee to push your balance even higher without you charging a single item. I know this sounds depressing, and believe me it is! In the graph below is a piece of a credit card statement, notice the balance, minimum payment, due date, and how long it can take to pay off the current balance.

Ex: **BALANCE: $5,606.45**
Minimum Payment: $113.00

If you make no additional charges using this card and each month you pay...	You will pay off the balance shown on this statement in about...	And you will end up paying an estimated total of...
Only the minimum payment	17 years	$11,731
$192	3 years	$6,897 (Savings = $4,834)

Now let us discuss how to pay them off much sooner. One thing you can do, if you have multiple credit cards, is consolidate them into a one lump sum payment. There are companies out there that will help you do this. They pay off your cards, and then you pay them one monthly payment, that is usually lower than the minimum payments of all your cards together. In August of 1997, I moved from New York State to South Carolina. Between my wife and I, we had 5 credit cards. I devised a plan so that in one year I had paid off 3 of these cards. After 2 years I had it down to one. It took me about 3 more years to pay off the final card. So this is how I did it.

Let us say we have 3 credit cards. Card #1 has a balance of $4,000.00 with a minimum payment of $84.00 a month. Card #2 has a balance of $1,200.00 with a minimum payment of $35.00 a month. Card #3 has a balance of $900.00 with a minimum payment $30.00 a month. So for all 3 cards the minimum payment is $149.00 a month, divided by 4 is $37.25 a week. You need to set aside $37.25 per week in your budget to make the minimum payments on all your cards.

One thing about becoming debt free is to take small steps. Do not try to over extend yourself and think that this is quick and easy. It is a lot easier to get into debt than to get out. So we are going to attack small bills first and then work our way up to the bigger bills.

One thing about paying the minimum payment on credit cards is that the minimum payment keeps going down as the balance goes down, and we do not keep charging on them. Unlike a car loan where the payment is always the same until the loan is paid off. So we are going to attack the card with the smallest balance first. Card #3 has a balance of $900.00 with a minimum payment of $30.00. As you were able to save $1,000.00 for the emergency fund, you are now going to help out card #3's payment the same way. So whatever you have left over from your paycheck every week, it is to be put into the credit card fund. Let us say we only have $10.00 left over every week. That adds up to $40.00 extra that can be applied to card #3's payment. When the bill comes in for card #3, and the minimum payment is $30.00, we are now going to apply the $40.00 extra. This will make your payment $70.00 for that month. Next month when card #3's bill comes in, perhaps the minimum payment has gone down to $28.00. We will keep our minimum payment at $30.00. Maybe next month we have $50.00 left over from our weekly paychecks. That makes card #3's payment of $30.00 + $50.00, which equals $80.00. Remember to just make the minimum payments on cards #1 and #2. As you are still setting aside $149.00 per month for all credit card payments. When the minimum payments on cards #1 and #2 go down, just pay the minimum payments. The extra is to be applied to card #3. Example; Card #1's minimum payment was $84.00 and is now $80.00. Card #2's minimum payment was $35.00 and is now $30.00. The

$4.00 extra from card #1 and the $5.00 extra from card #2 is to be applied to card #3. So card #3's payment is now $30.00, (original minimum payment) + $9.00 from cards #1 and #2, + $40.00 from left over weekly paychecks, which comes to a total of $79.00. Another way to apply extra money to paying off a credit card is making the budget plan work in your favor. The plan is set up for 4 weeks in a month. There is an extra week every few months, which adds up to 4 per year. So 4 times a year there is 5 weeks in a month. Now when this happens you can make a huge payment. All the money that is put into the weekly budget can now be applied to card #3's payment. So let us add it up; card #3's minimum payment of $30.00, + $119.00 from cards #1 and #2, + house payment of $257.50, + car payment of $105.00, + insurance payment of $55.00, + electric payment of $50.00, + phone and internet payment of $30.00, + miscellaneous payment of $50.00, and $10.00 from left over paychecks, which brings the total to $706.50. WOW! What a payment. So keep doing this process until card #3 is paid off. Congratulations! You have just paid off a credit card. At this point it might be a good idea to destroy this credit card and cancel it from the bank, so that you will not be tempted to use this card again. Also, you need to celebrate and reward yourself, take yourself out to the movies or to your favorite restaurant. This is a major accomplishment. Now it is time to attack credit card #2. Perhaps now the balance has gone down to $1,000.00 with a minimum payment of $29.00. We are going to keep the original payment of $35.00, + card #3's original payment of $30.00, + $40.00 of left over weekly paychecks. Now let us say that card #1's minimum payment is now down to $72.00. The original payment was $84.00. Pay $72.00, (minimum payment) to card #1, and take the extra $12.00 and apply to card #2's payment. With all the extra money, card #2's payment is now $117.00. Keep doing this until card #2 is paid off. Plus you may get another 5 week gift to help you along. Congratulations! You have just paid off your 2nd credit card. It is probably a good idea to destroy this card and cancel it from the bank. Once again reward yourself. It is good to have this feeling of accomplishment. Now it is time to attack card #1. At this time card #1's balance is down to let us say $3,000.00 with a minimum payment of $65.00. We are going to take the entire credit card fund of $149.00 + whatever is left over from weekly paychecks to make payments. Let us say once again it is $40.00 for a month. Add this to the $149.00 for a total of $189.00. So $189.00 is this month's payment to card #1. Keep doing this until credit card #1 is paid off. If you should happen to have just one credit card, then do the process of what I said for credit card #1. Congratulations! You have just paid off another credit card and have just completed STEP #3. Once again go out and celebrate and reward yourself. Instead of destroying this card it might be a good idea to keep this card. If you do, make sure that when you charge on this card you can pay it off each month. Credit cards are needed sometimes to reserve hotel rooms or to get rental cars. As I said before, this is a big step and will take a few years to complete. You now have an extra $149.00 a month. You have just taken a huge step to being debt free, and believe me, this is a great feeling.

CHAPTER 5 STEP #4
LIVING EXPENSES
PHASE ONE

The next step is to save one month's worth of living expenses. To determine how much this is, we will need to consult our budget plan.

House Payment $257.50/wk x 4 = $1,030.00/mo

Car Payment $105.00/wk x 4 = $420.00/mo

Insurance $55.00/wk x 4 = $220.00/mo

Electric $50.00/wk x 4 = $200.00/mo

Phone & Internet $30.00/wk x 4 = $120.00/mo

Miscellaneous $50.00/wk x 4 = $200.00/mo

Groceries $100.00/wk x 4 = $400.00/mo

Gasoline $50.00/wk x 4 = $200.00/mo

Other Essentials $40.00/wk x 4 = $160.00/mo

Weekly Expenses $737.50 x 4 = $2,950.00 Monthly Expenses

So on top of our $1,000.00 emergency fund, we will need to save an additional $2,950.00. This will bring our total savings to $3,950.00. This money would be used in the case of a job loss, medical leave, or just in between jobs. Basically if you have no income for a month, this will help you to survive. You need to try and avoid using those tempting credit cards.

CHAPTER 6 STEP #5 CONSUMER DEBT

Step #5 is to pay off all remaining consumer debt. This would consist of retail store credit cards, lay-a-ways, hospital bills, or bank loans on various projects such as renovations. This should be an easy step to complete. You might be able to skip right over this step, if you do not have any of these debts.

CHAPTER 7 STEP #6 LIVING EXPENSES PHASE TWO

This step sets us up to really increase our savings. We now need to add 3 months worth of living expenses. We have previously determined, in chapter 5, that it takes $2,950.00 to equal one month's worth of living expenses. To increase the living expenses to 3 months we will need to multiply $2,950.00 by 3 which come to $7,850.00. This would be added to the overall savings of $3,950.00, and this will bring the total to $11,800.00. Once again, this will help you to survive, if you lose your job, need a medical leave, or just in between jobs. Basically if you had no income for 3 months, or longer, you could survive.

CHAPTER 8 STEP #7
THE CAR

It is time to pay off the car early. The first thing we can do is round the car payment up to the next $50.00 amount. For example; our payment is $420.00 a month. So rounding it up to the next $50.00 amount would make the payment at $450.00 a month. That would make the payment on the weekly budget go from $105.00 to $112.50, only an increase of $7.50 a week. This would also change your 60 month loan to a 47 month loan, and save you at least $1,000.00 in interest. The second thing we can do is make one extra car payment a year. Do not forget our weekly budget plan is set up for 4 weeks in a month. 4 times a year there is 5 weeks in a month. There is an extra week every few months; which adds up to 4 extra weeks in a year. So those 4 extra weeks translates to one extra month of payments per year. The third thing you should do is make sure you never skip a payment under any circumstances. Skipping car payments adds interest to your car loan and it can also hurt your credit score. The fourth thing we can do is make ½ payments every 2 weeks. It is said that this can take 6 months off of your loan. I do not have any proof of this, and I am not sure this works. Therefore I do not recommend this. Now that your car is paid off!

Your have just taken another major step towards being debt free. Plus you have an extra $105.00 a week in your take home pay. It is time for another celebration and a reward to you. Keep this in mind that throughout all this you should be always saving for retirement, and always adding to your savings.

CHAPTER 9 STEP #8 MORTGAGE PAYOFF

Step #8 is the final hurdle, and the final line to cross to be debt free. It is a very big step, but knowing that you have come this far there is nothing too big to accomplish. So now we are going to pay off the mortgage. This is the only debt that is considered to be good debt. Before I paid off my mortgage I went and spoke with about 10 different people that I know and respect from all different walks of life. Once I had the money to do this, my question I put to these people was should I pay off my house or not? 7 out 10 said yes, and that convinced me that this was the thing to do.

It is best before even starting a mortgage to find out what would be an affordable, or how much of a mortgage you should have. It should not exceed 2 ½ times your annual salary. We determined that the average annual salary is $49,600. So 2 ½ times this amount would come to $124,000. So if you make around $49,600 a year you should not buy a home that exceeds $124,000. Now let us pay it off quickly! 1. Pay a little extra every month. You could try paying an extra 1/12 of the already monthly payment. Our monthly payment, according to our set budget plan, is $1,030.00 a month. To figure out how much an extra 1/12 would be. Take the $1,030.00 and divide it by 12. This comes to $85.83. We are just going to make it $85.00. Now add the $85.00 to the $1,030.00, and this comes to $1,115.00 a month. This also raises the weekly budget from $257.50 to $278.75, an increase of $21.25. Do not forget, you do not have car payments or credit card payments. Doing this will save you 10's of thousands of dollars in interest over the years. 2. Make one extra payment per year; this follows the same rule we did in the car payment. 3. You can make ½ payments every 2 weeks. Make sure you check with you bank before doing this, some banks will allow it and some will not. I tried doing this and it did not work for me. 4. You can refinance your home at a lower interest rate. This may lower your monthly payment. If so you should continue with the same payment as you had before. You may want to pick a different mortgage plan. Instead of paying for 30 years; you may want to go to 20 or 15 years. Just remember this; fewer years, bigger payments and less interest; more years, smaller payments and more interest. One thing you do not want to do is sign up for an ACCEDERALETED PAYMENT PLAN!!! This will lock you in with absolutely no freedom. If for whatever reason you had to skip or miss a payment this would really damage you in your finances and you would have a lot of catching up to do. So know what you can afford and pick the plan that best suits you. 5. Should you receive a large sum of money through an inheritance, law suit, lottery or gambling winnings, or an investment payout? You can use this to pay off your mortgage.

CONGRATULATIONS! You have just reached a major milestone in your life. You have become DEBT FREE! Oh what a feeling! Financial freedom; there is almost not a better feeling in the world. All your worries and burdens are simply just vanished. This is a cause for a major celebration with a party and fireworks do it you certainly earned it.

CHAPTER 10 THE CONCLUSION

After completing all the steps to becoming DEBT FREE, it is easy to keep yourself there. Reason being you will have more money to work with, and you will have a completely different mindset. You will make wiser choices and you will have your spending under control. You may want to hire yourself a financial advisor, which can guide you and set you up for retirement. You can look into making smart investments such as gold and silver, 401K, IRA, high interest savings accounts, stocks, bonds, annuities, and investments in reliable companies. You need to have a varied portfolio. You need to make your retirement fund as large, and strong as possible.

One thing more I wanted to mention is concerning the budget. As you work it and pay your bills from it, there comes a time when some funds come up short. Or sometimes there is extra money built up in one of the other funds. You can take from the extra fund and pay the one that is short. Or if you have some extra money in some of the varied funds and you are wondering where to apply this money. I would suggest putting into your savings account or go out and treat yourself. After all, you have worked hard for a long time and you certainly deserve it!

Remember to take small steps; do not skip over steps or try to rush them. You have got to teach yourself to stay focused and to never give up hope! After all, it took me about 15 years to accomplish this. I just pray that GOD will truly bless you and keep you on the path to success.

ACKNOWLEDGEMENTS

CROWN MINISTRIES THE MONEY MAP

REALSIMPLE.COM

PAYOFF.COM

SMARTASSET.COM

THE WASHINGTON POST

THEBALANCECAREERS.COM

CREDITKARMA.COM

DAVE RAMSEY

REVIEWS

I have known the Surine's for several years. I have gotten to know Dyke and his family very well. In fact they have become part of my family. I actually prayed that he would write a help book on finances. It has come to pass here in this book. But I am writing this review in reference to my personal testimony, as Dyke finished the book, I was blessed to have read the final print. I have been debt free for many years and thought I had a hold on it. As I read his book I found holes in my finances that needed to be corrected. This book is anointed and appointed by GOD to bless and help all. I believe that this book can pull you out of poverty and bring you to great prosperity, and lead you to a better life of being debt free. I believe that there will be a sequel to this book that will go deeper into finances. I thank GOD for Dyke and his family. This is a #1 read in my life.

- Ric Lyons Freedom Fighters

www.ingramcontent.com/pod-product-compliance
Lightning Source LLC
Chambersburg PA
CBHW071326200326
41520CB00013B/2874